THIS BOOK BELONGS TO:

Hello, Great One!

Please leave a review because we would love to know your thoughts, opinions, and feedback to create better products for you!

We appreciate your support, Gracias.

What Is a Vision Board?

A vision board is a unique collection of quotes, pictures, inspirational & motivational sayings, or other items that will help you focus on your aspirations, aims and dreams.

Why Use Affirmations and Quotes?

What you tell yourself matters. Your feelings can be influenced by the words you use and the thoughts you have.

You're more likely to behave in the direction of your goals when you're feeling happy.

Taking action encourages you to have confidence in yourself and your goals.

By focusing on inspiring words, quotes, and success affirmations, you can change your thinking.

You can decide to pick vision board quotes (affirmations, motivational & inspirational) that are relevant to you - cut and paste/pin it in a place/position that will often get your attention.

Every sunset is an opportunity to reset.

GRL PWR

YOU ARE *stronger* THAN YOU THINK YOU ARE

You were built for something wonderful.

THERE ARE BIG OPPORTUNITIES COMING TOWARDS ME.

The hard things will get easier

JUST KEEP GOING

MOVE
FORWARD
GOOD THINGS
ARE →
UP AHEAD

BE AWE SOME

you're never too old to begin

"Take time to do what makes your soul happy.

Enjoy Everyday

REMINDER:
FIND PERSPECTIVE IN
THE SHADES IN BETWEEN.

Today's Affirmation

You always deserve Everything you desire

LOVE MYSELF

TRUST YOURSELF

Start your
journey as
they you
want to.

Dear Monday

I'm loved

I'm blessed

I'm happy

I'll do my best

I promise

Be proud of
yourself
for how hard
you're trying

Today's
Affirmation

Be positive

Be happy

Be You

ON THIS DAY
I will

Trust in God

Be less worried

Use kind words

Positive thinking

MY BODY
MY CHOICE

DO YOUR THING

THE ROAD AHEAD HAS

WON DER FUL

THINGS IN STORE FOR ME.

Affirmation

I wake up today with strength in my heart and clarity in my mind.

EVERYTHING IS POSSIBLE BELIEVE!

IF NOT, NOW WHEN?

BE THE PERSON (YOU WANT TO HAVE IN your life

You have always been enough

You Can Move Mountains

STAY STRONG & POWER ON

I believe in you

TRUST THE TIMING OF YOUR LIFE

i am Confident

attract positivity

HAKUNA MATATA

SELF CARE IS A PRIORITY AND Necessity NOT A LUXURY

you got this

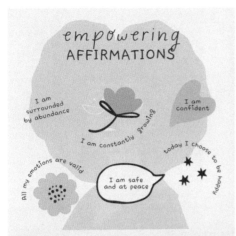

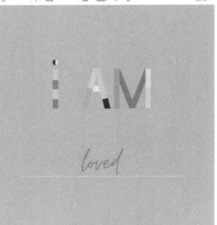

EVERYDAY ✦ ✦

AFFIRMATIONS

- ✦ I AM COMPLETE AS I AM
- ✦ POSITIVITY SURROUNDS ME
- ✦ MY FEELINGS ARE VALID
- ✦ I AM WORTHY OF LOVE
- ✦ TODAY IS FULL OF OPPORTUNITY

hello
Sunshine

CONGRA
TULATION

Happiness
is a
Choice

YOU'RE
BRILLIANT

CARPE
DIEM

YOU are
OUT
of this
WORLD

I Hope you Feel beautiful Today

be the BEST version of ★ you

No DRAMA please

boss
BABE

HELLO
gorgeous

Stay WILD & free ♡

YES! women can

LOVE YOUR BODY

YOU CAN!

make your own ADVENTURE

HELLO MONDAY

YOU ARE a WARRIOR

YOU WILL DO GREAT

BRAVE GIRL

EVERY THING WILL BE OKAY

-THE-
BEST
project
YOU WILL EVER
WORK ON
is your self

LET YOUR
IDEAS
bloom

LOVE WHO
YOU ARE

THINK
POSitive

BE HAPPY

keep life SIMPLE

ENJOY EVERY MOMENT

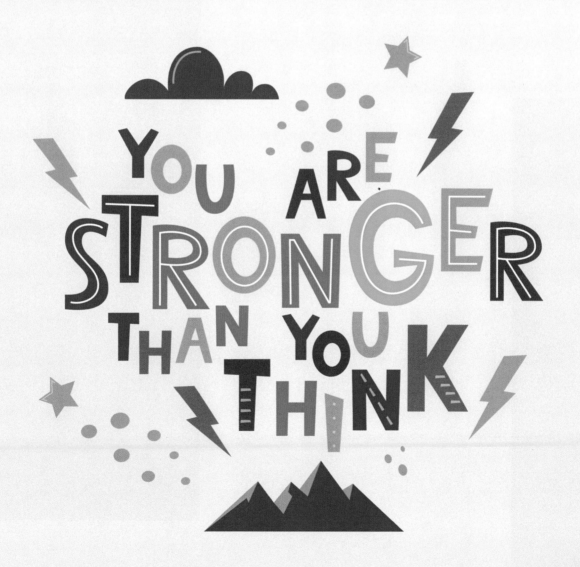

YOU ARE STRONGER THAN YOU THINK

POSITIVE QUOTES BUNDLE

HERO

NEVER Give up

YOU ARE AMAZING

Made in the USA
Las Vegas, NV
28 December 2023

83637296R00024